MONKEY MIND ANXIETY CURE AFFIRMATIONS, MEDITATION & HYPNOSIS:

How to Stop Worrying, Kill Fear, Rewire Your Brain, and Change Your Anxious Thoughts to Start Living a Stress Free Life

DREW MCARTHUR

© Copyright 2019 by Drew McArthur - All rights reserved.

The following book is reproduced below with the goal of providing information that is as accurate and reliable as possible. Regardless, purchasing this book can be seen as consent to the fact that both the publisher and the author of this book are in no way experts on the topics discussed within and that any recommendations or suggestions that are made herein are for entertainment purposes only. Professionals should be consulted as needed prior to undertaking any of the action endorsed herein.

This declaration is deemed fair and valid by both the American Bar Association and the Committee of Publishers Association and is legally binding throughout the United States.

Furthermore, the transmission, duplication or reproduction of any of the following work including specific information will be considered an illegal act irrespective of if it is done electronically or in print. This extends to creating a secondary or tertiary copy of the work or a recorded copy and is only allowed with express written consent from the Publisher. All additional right reserved.

The information in the following pages is broadly considered to be a truthful and accurate account of facts, and as such any inattention, use or misuse of the information in question by the reader will render any resulting actions solely under their purview. There are no scenarios in which the publisher or the original author of this work can be in any fashion deemed *liable for any hardship or damages that may befall them after undertaking information described herein.*

Additionally, the information in the following pages is intended only for informational purposes and should thus be thought of as universal. As befitting its nature, it is presented without assurance regarding its prolonged validity or interim quality. Trademarks that are mentioned are done without written consent and can in no way be considered an endorsement from the trademark holder.

All by Drew McArthur on Amazon & Audible

Affirmations, Meditation, & Hypnosis For Positivity & A Success Mindset:

Power Of Thought To Create A Millionaire Mind, Manifest Wealth, Abundance, Better Relationships, & Form Positive Habits Now

Rewire Your Brain Affirmations, Meditation, & Hypnosis For Confidence, Motivation, & Discipline:

Increase Focus, Productivity, Willpower, Self Esteem, & Eliminate Distraction & Procrastination Habits

Step-By-Step Motivational Goal Setting Course For Life Mastery:

How To Change Your Brain, Set Your Vision, And Get Everything You Want To Have Your Best Year Ever

Monkey Mind Cure Affirmations, Meditation & Hypnosis:

How to Stop Worrying, Kill Fear, Rewire Your Brain, and Change Your Anxious Thoughts to Start Living a Stress and Anxiety-Free Life

Think Happy Thoughts: Affirmations and Meditation for Positive Thinking, Learned Optimism and a Happy Brain

Unlock the Advantage of the Happiness Habit and Project the Power of Positive Energy

Millionaire Money Mindset: Affirmations, Meditation, & Hypnosis

Using Positive Thinking Psychology to Train Your Mind to Grow Wealth, Think like the New Rich and Take the Secret Fastlane to Success

Contents

Introduction	ix
Fostering Positive Thinking	1
Conquering Inadequacy	11
Financial Concerns	25
Handling Professional, Work, & Business Stress	41
Personal Relationships	55
Overcoming Social Anxiety	69
Physical Body & Health	87
Cultivating Optimism	95
All by Drew McArthur on Amazon & Audible	107

Introduction

The monkey mind goes from worry to worry, constantly unsettled. If it's not worrying about one thing, it's worrying about another, but one thing remains constant—it is always worrying. This creates endless cycles of worry, stress, and anxiety that diminish the quality of our lives. It's hard to think straight, think clearly, make necessary decisions, perform well at work, feel confident, be present and happy in our personal lives, or just enjoy life in general without a constant fear of what's next.

Introduction

So much of our worries and fears come from insecurity around the present and the future—future concerns about our finances, health, relationships, and career. And then there's just the general feelings of inadequacy, pessimism, and social anxiety.

Your mindset makes all the difference. Disempowering thoughts can make you feel helpless, and hopeless. And these negative thoughts are often rooted in our subconscious, so we don't even realize the psychological damage we're doing to ourselves. But training your brain to be positive, optimistic, and expect good things to happen to you and for you, can be the difference between seeing success, and not seeing success.

And a successful life is a life of mental peace and optimism that stems from knowing and believing that everything is okay right now, and everything is going to be okay in the future. And that begins (and

Introduction

ends) in the mind—shaping and training it to think how you want it to think.

When we retrain our brains to know that we are capable of handling any situation that comes our way, and to expect good things to happen to us, we can finally free ourselves from the negativity of anxiety, and living in constant fear and pessimism.

One very effective way to do this is by using affirmations. Affirmations can quite literally rewire your mind, by physically affecting the neural pathways in your brain. Affirmations, when spoken coupled with the feeling one would feel if they honestly believed them to be true, can be extremely powerful tools in improving and changing your life.

The order of the sections and categories of affirmations is as follows:

- Fostering Positive Thinking

Introduction

- Physical Body & Health
- Financial Concerns
- Overcoming Social Anxiety
- Conquering Inadequacy
- Personal Relationships
- Handling Professional, Work, & Business Stress
- Creating Optimism

You can go directly to the section that you need most or just let this play from beginning to end. Some sections are shorter than others. So you can also select the section of your choice based on what you have time for at that given time. Because this is designed for audio and continuous listening, there is no conclusion for this audiobook.

Now, let's see how you can make the most out of this...

You can use this audiobook as affirmations, meditation, or hypnosis. If you choose to use it as affirmations, I suggest that you pick a time and a place where you will feel completely confident speaking each affirmation out loud. Maybe for you, that's your bathroom in front of your mirror before bed every night. Maybe it's your living room when the kids are away at soccer practice. Maybe it's your car on your commute on your way to work. No matter where you choose to recite your affirmations, remember that the whole point of this is to ingrain positive, strong thoughts in your head. So, make sure your body language reflects that also. Depending upon where you are, stand up straight, or sit up straight while you speak each statement aloud. Make sure your shoulders are back and your head is up. The confidence in your body needs to be in alignment with the confidence in your words and thoughts in order for this to work. You cannot speak powerful statements and think positive thoughts, while having a slumped, unconfident, disempowered posture in your body.

Introduction

If you would like to use this as meditation, before you begin, find a quiet place where you will remain undisturbed for the entire length of the audio. Then, remove all distractions. Turn off your phone, eliminate as much noise as possible, close the door to where ever you are, and alert anyone around you not to disturb you for the next two hours. When you're ready to begin, find a comfortable position, either sitting up or laying down, and be sure to remove all physical tension from your body. Choose a position that is comfortable enough for you to allow the muscles of your body to relax, but that will also ensure that you stay awake. Many people like to sit with their legs crossed and their hands resting palm up or down on their knees. Some people prefer to lay down on their backs, with their arms palms up, by their sides. Choose whichever is best for you. Then, once you are settled into position, you can either choose a spot to look at

Introduction

and drop your eyelids and soften your gaze, or you can close your eyes altogether. Then, begin clearing your mind of all past, present, and future thoughts and worries, and deepen your relaxed state by slowing your breathing to long, deep breaths, fully inhaling, then fully exhaling. When you feel you are adequately relaxed, begin the audio. If you like, you can just listen to the audio and let the words seep into your mind and your consciousness, or you can repeat them in your head during the pauses.

Lastly, if you would like to use this as hypnosis, simply start the audio and let it play when you go to bed, allowing the words to embed themselves into your subconscious as you fall asleep.

It doesn't matter how you choose to use this audio, as all of the methods can be effective for you, and make a noticeable difference in your default state of mind and

Introduction

your future success. The ideal scenario may even be to use a combination of all three. That way, you can not only consciously absorb these thoughts, but you can also simultaneously subconsciously absorb them as well. The most important thing is to be consistent. Whatever you do, make sure you do it every day—even multiple times a day if you have time. You can begin your day with affirmations, and end it with meditation and hypnosis. But just keep doing it. Change will not happen overnight. It will take time to reprogram your mind for success, but I assure you, it will be well worth the effort.

Don't worry about looking or sounding weird to other people. Don't worry about what other people may think of you. Whenever you feel strange or uncomfortable about doing this, just remember why you are doing this and think about your goals. If you need help setting goals, I have

Introduction

a program available on Audible that can help you with that task.

I also have several other affirmations audio programs that will help you continue your quest towards habitual positive thinking. So be sure to check out my other titles on Audible and Amazon.

And now, let us begin. Welcome to the next step in becoming a better, happier, more effective version of yourself. Are you ready?

Fostering Positive Thinking

1. I am in complete control of how I feel today.
2. I choose to be happy today no matter what happens or does not happen.
3. I live my life the way I want to live it.
4. Everything that happens to me happens for me.
5. Today, I will do everything within my control to have the best day I possibly can.

6. I have the power to make today a wonderful day.
7. I possess everything I need to succeed.
8. I am stronger today than I was yesterday.
9. I am not inferior to others and I will not feel inferior to others.
10. The way I live my life is an inspiration to other people.
11. I choose the path I walk today and every day, and I only detour if I consciously decide to.
12. I write all the chapters in the story of my life and I love each and every one.
13. I only say yes to people or things I want to say yes to.
14. I deserve happiness and peace, and I attract happiness and peace.
15. I have exciting personal goals and dreams and I deserve to achieve them.

16. Seeing others achieve success makes me feel inspired, not jealous.
17. I am unique and I am happy with my uniqueness.
18. Everything that happens in my life is for my ultimate benefit.
19. When things don't work out the way I want them to, I learn from it and move onwards and upwards.
20. Every no just gets me closer to a yes.
21. I believe fully in myself and all the things I am capable of accomplishing.
22. I love myself for who I am today, while I work on becoming a better me tomorrow.
23. I have complete confidence in my own decisions.
24. I choose to only spend my energy on the present task in front of me

in the present moment in the present day.
25. I save tomorrow's cares for tomorrow and only focus on making today a great day.
26. I am in complete control of my mood, no matter what the mood is of other people around me.
27. I honor my commitments to myself and others.
28. I replace negative thoughts with positive thoughts and repeat them until they become effortless.
29. My thoughts and feelings are just as important as everyone else's thoughts and feelings.
30. I can easily ignore negativity because it has no place in my life.
31. Today and every day, I think kind thoughts because my mind seeks peace.
32. I am in complete control of my life and I know what I am doing.

33. I graciously accept praise and compliments from others because I am worthy of praise and compliments.
34. I am completely comfortable asking for help if I feel I need it.
35. Today is another opportunity for me to become a better version of me.
36. I become more intelligent every day because I open myself up to learning opportunities.
37. I am comfortable with myself and the person I am right now.
38. As long as I know and understand where I am going, it doesn't matter if anyone else does.
39. The path I choose to walk is the best path for me.
40. I choose to smile today regardless of how I feel.
41. My mind is mine to control, and my thoughts are mine to enjoy.

42. I always have the energy to do what I need to do and accomplish what I need to accomplish.
43. Whatever I have is enough for me and I don't need what anyone else has.
44. I attract positive people who help me to stay positive with my thoughts.
45. I love myself as I am now and I continuously find reasons to love myself more.
46. I am passionate and driven, and great achievements lie ahead for me.
47. I have the ability to build the kind of life I want to live.
48. I focus on the good things in life, no matter what is going on around me.
49. Success is not something to be feared but something to be embraced.

50. I possess enough inner strength for me to achieve the goals I set for myself.
51. I do not set roadblocks in a clear road but instead, I go forth with confidence.
52. Time is on my side and I will take as much of it as I need to reach my goals.
53. My life's journey operates on its own schedule, not anybody else's.
54. The timeline I take to accomplish my goals is unique for me.
55. Life is a gift, and I will enjoy my journey, every step of the way.
56. Life is to be lived daily, and I will live my best today, whatever my best is today.
57. I openly give to others and I also openly receive from others.
58. Change is good, and I embrace its ability to help me grow and improve.

59. I easily work through my stress and enjoy the peace that is on the other side.
60. Life is a wonderful adventure and I am ready to go where ever it takes me.
61. I am confident, strong, and able to take care of myself.
62. While I am always striving for improvement, today, I am all that I need to be.
63. Life is beautiful and so am I.
64. Everything I do brings me closer to being a better, happier version of myself.
65. Mistakes are nothing but learning opportunities that show us a better way forward.
66. I possess amazing talents that I use every day.
67. My potential for success is limitless.
68. I am strong and courageous and I

confidently defend myself and my beliefs.
69. I possess good, productive daily habits that benefit me.
70. The things that happen today will make my life better tomorrow.
71. I choose happiness right now, and I find fun, joy, and excitement in every day.
72. I experience and appreciate the joys of today, while anticipating the joys of tomorrow.
73. I am capable of finding a solution to any problem.
74. I approve of who I am and what I am doing right now in my life, and that is enough for me.
75. I have complete trust in my decisions because I know me better than anyone else ever will.

Conquering Inadequacy

1. I am a person of value and I deserve to be treated with kindness.
2. Perfection is impossible but I will be my best self today and every day.
3. I have flaws and they are what make me unique.
4. I have the ability to learn new things quickly and easily.
5. I am powerful enough to get through any situation.

6. I deserve to feel good and I only allow positivity in my mind.
7. Every day, I am changing and growing into a better version of me.
8. The person I am becoming is a wonderful person who deserves the best in life.
9. I am a worthy person and I deserve all the good things that happen to me.
10. I choose to focus on excitement over my future instead of regret over my past.
11. My decisions are intelligent and well thought out, and I will defend them.
12. People love me and I deserve that love.
13. I have the capacity to gain all the knowledge I need in this life.
14. All the things I need for success are easily within my grasp.

15. I am the best person for the task before me.
16. I trust myself to be able to produce great work.
17. I have the strength to work through any struggle I encounter.
18. I feel my inner strength growing every day.
19. My body has the capacity to do many wonderful things.
20. I am constantly amazed by what I am capable of.
21. I am a persistent person who never stops short of my goals.
22. I am steadily growing into the ideal version of myself.
23. I refuse to feel inferior because no one can make me feel that way.
24. I feel worthy of receiving all the amazing things that life has to offer.
25. I have the power to choose what I become in life.

26. I fully embrace and believe in my decisions.
27. I am good enough for today, and I am working on being better tomorrow.
28. There are no obstacles I cannot overcome because I am strong and resilient.
29. The job of liking me belongs to no one else but me.
30. Temporary failure is nothing more than a stepping stone that leads me down a better path.
31. I talk with confidence in my voice and I believe what I say.
32. I confidently say no when I need to protect my best interest.
33. It is okay for me to either agree or disagree with the opinions of others.
34. No one can defeat me.
35. I choose to love myself.

36. I appreciate and love myself for who I am inside and out.
37. I always receive compliments and I deserve to receive them.
38. I am capable of achieving any goal I want to achieve.
39. I am a unique individual and I enjoy my uniqueness.
40. My dreams are just as valid as anyone else's dreams.
41. My dreams deserve just as much attention as anyone else's dreams.
42. I am intelligent and wise and more than capable of making good choices.
43. I am capable of doing anything I set my mind to.
44. Everything I need to make today wonderful is already inside of me.
45. I have nothing to prove to anyone.
46. I fully accept myself for who I am.
47. I am fully ready to face any challenge that comes my way.

48. I deserve the place I hold in this world.
49. The world is a better place because I exist in it.
50. The world needs my gifts and talents and I am ready to give it to them.
51. My life has a special and unique destiny that the world needs to experience.
52. I am dedicated to fully realizing my limitless potential.
53. I have already made many accomplishments and I am proud of every one of them.
54. The best of what I have to offer is still to come.
55. I am completely open to giving and receiving love.
56. Although material riches are coming my way, material things do not define me.

57. I am still a whole person without flashy, material possessions.
58. I approve of myself and how I am living my life.
59. I am not perfect and that is good because perfect is boring.
60. I don't have to be perfect to be loved or valued.
61. My flaws make me more interesting and loveable.
62. I treat myself in the wonderful way I deserve to be treated.
63. I only allow others to treat me in the wonderful way I deserve to be treated.
64. I am very proud of all the things I accomplished today.
65. I am an amazing person and I will be even more amazing tomorrow.
66. I am an extraordinary person and I deserve extraordinary things to happen in my life.
67. It is okay to make mistakes

because I learn from them and move onwards and upwards.
68. I approve of my life and the wise life choices I make.
69. I am smart enough to make great choices in life.
70. I believe in myself and the extraordinary things I can do.
71. I am complete and valuable just the way I am, but I always choose to grow.
72. I always go forward with confidence, no matter what others think.
73. I have purpose and value within me.
74. I always do my very best and my best is enough.
75. I am smart enough to sharpen my skills if needed.
76. I deserve to be happy and I do what I need to to cultivate that feeling within me.

77. I can fully rely on myself for all the things I need because I am strong enough.
78. I am strong enough to seek help when needed, which is a sign of strength, not weakness.
79. I can find the solution to any problem.
80. I have just as much to offer the world as the next person does.
81. I have the courage to make every day a great day.
82. The power to make my life the way I want it to be is within me and I will use it.
83. I am aware of the potential living inside of me.
84. I am my own best source of love and affection.
85. I can make the world a better place just by being in it every day.
86. My presence is enough to bring light and love into the world.

87. I am strong and capable and I can do anything I set my mind to.
88. My talents need to be shared with the world.
89. I am always moving forward despite any obstacle that shows up.
90. My intelligence will take me anywhere I want to go.
91. I am doing my best today and that is all I expect from myself.
92. I have enough energy to take on the world and create my best life.
93. I have infinite potential to succeed and absolute faith in my abilities.
94. I am confident in my ability to survive and thrive with grace and humility.
95. I deserve to receive love from the people around me.
96. I become stronger in my abilities every day.

97. Every endeavor I embark upon is destined for success.
98. I feel sufficient peace to live a calm and happy life.
99. Today will be a better day than yesterday because I am a better person than I was yesterday.
100. The people closest to me know me for who I am and love me for it.
101. Today will bring happiness and joy to me because I deserve it.
102. I have the power to make my life wonderful.
103. I possess the outstanding ability to make all my dreams come true.
104. There is no such thing as failure, only opportunities to learn and grow.
105. I write my own definition of success and I am living it daily.
106. I have a good heart and I always give love to others.

107. I give my best effort in every situation.
108. I take care of myself because I am worth it.
109. I have the confidence to do what needs to be accomplished today.
110. I have the energy to do what needs to be accomplished today.
111. I have the resilience to do what needs to be accomplished today.
112. I have the intelligence to do what needs to be accomplished today.
113. I have the resourcefulness to do what needs to be accomplished today.
114. I am secure in what I want and how to get there.
115. I have unconditional love for who I am and for who I am becoming.
116. My world is in my control and I can change what I don't like.
117. I love my body the way it is and I am always working to improve it.

118. I respect myself completely and I know what I deserve.
119. I deserve to have healthy romantic relationships.
120. My past is nothing more than lessons I have learned that make me a better version of me.
121. I consciously decide to think only positive thoughts about myself.
122. My mind is a wonderful well of ideas and I owe it to the world to share it.
123. I am always climbing to new heights of professional success.
124. I move forward in the face of doubt because I know what I am truly capable of.
125. I move forward in the face of fear because I know what I am truly capable of.
126. I move forward in the face of rejection because I know what I am truly capable of.

127. My opinions and ideas are valued in my professional world.
128. I will pass any test that comes before me.
129. I can get through any trial or tribulation that shows up in my life.

Financial Concerns

1. The abundance of money I have brings comfort to myself and my loved ones.
2. I feel secure in the abundance of money I have in my bank account.
3. Money is a good and powerful tool, and I use it for good and powerful things.
4. I am comforted in knowing that all my financial needs are met.
5. Financial abundance comes to me when I look for it.

6. More money comes to me when I ask for it and claim it.
7. I use my wealth to make a better life for myself and others.
8. I handle my finances wisely and intelligently.
9. I am a magnet for prosperity, and money flows into my life freely.
10. I am a master of money, and my money always grows and multiplies.
11. Money is a never-ending resource that constantly flows to me in abundance.
12. I have more than enough money to meet my needs and desires.
13. I will always have more than enough money to meet my needs and desires.
14. I am a worthy person with worthy talents and abilities, and I deserve to make more money.

15. Wealth and abundance are my way of life.
16. Although I work to have more, I am happy with what I have.
17. I am open and willing to receive all the wealth that is possible for me in this life.
18. I am constantly discovering new avenues for making money.
19. I have unlimited income and unending wealth.
20. I am rich, and with my riches, I improve the lives of myself and my loved ones.
21. I am grateful to have enough money to ensure that I receive the best healthcare possible.
22. I am grateful to have enough money to ensure that my loved ones receive the best healthcare possible.
23. The things I do today will make me wealthier tomorrow.

24. I intentionally seek and pursue opportunities to increase my income.
25. I take action on money-making opportunities.
26. I follow through on money-making opportunities.
27. My nest egg is growing more and more each day.
28. I have more than enough money saved for my future.
29. I have more than enough money invested for my future.
30. I am wise with money and always discovering new ways to grow it.
31. I am confident, savvy investor.
32. I have complete mental peace around money.
33. I have complete emotional peace around money.
34. I have complete spiritual peace around money.

35. I have more money than I could have ever imagined.
36. I have more than enough money to take care of myself and my family.
37. I am constantly expanding my opportunities in life with the abundant riches that come to me.
38. I have a bright financial future.
39. I use the abundance of wealth that I have to make my dreams come true.
40. I have an abundant mindset and therefore live an abundant life.
41. I see the glass as half full and not half empty.
42. My wealth allows for amazing life experiences for me and my loved ones.
43. I sleep peacefully every night because I know my financial future is secure.
44. Money is good to talk about, good

to pursue, good to earn, and good to have.
45. Money is easy to talk about, easy to pursue, easy to earn, and easy to have.
46. I only feel positive thoughts, judgments, and emotions around money.
47. Wealth and ethics can coexist.
48. I am always able to easily pay my bills and have plenty leftover.
49. I am still a good person even though I am wealthy.
50. I am still a grounded person even though I am wealthy.
51. I am still a humble person even though I am wealthy.
52. I shamelessly live my life according to my personal income standards, not someone else's.
53. I proudly strive for abundance, even if no one else around me is doing so.

54. Money is a good and positive tool used to create a good quality of life.
55. I believe it is possible to be a good person and be rich at the same time.
56. I allow myself to earn and pursue more because it is my right.
57. It is my duty to do, be, and earn as much as I am capable of.
58. Money is a good thing to have in abundance.
59. Money creates opportunity, opportunity creates lifestyle, and lifestyle creates quality of life.
60. I have all the money I need to provide myself with all the things I need.
61. I have all the money I want to provide me with all the things I want.
62. I am attracted to money and money is attracted to me.

63. Money flows freely into my life and I freely accept it.
64. There is no limit to the amount of money I am capable of earning in my life.
65. I will have more money tomorrow than I do today.
66. I possess all the power I need to get the financial success I desire.
67. I have powerful skills and talents valuable enough to exchange for large amounts of money.
68. The more value I provide, the more money I make.
69. I remain focused on my pursuit of financial peace and wealth.
70. Every day is filled with new chances to make more money.
71. It is never too late for me to become more, achieve more, and acquire more.
72. My mind is open and accepting of new ways to financial freedom.

73. Each month, I have income flowing to me from multiple sources.
74. I am able to create excellent business opportunities that will bring me financial freedom.
75. My income far exceeds my expenses.
76. I earn more than enough money to live the life of my dreams.
77. My financial abundance allows me to help others in need.
78. Whenever I want something, I can pay for it in full.
79. I look over my finances with peace because I see abundance.
80. I look over my finances with confidence because I see abundance.
81. I look over my finances with calmness because I see abundance.
82. I choose to live a rich life and I

accept the money to be able to do so.
83. I have all the power I need to build the financial freedom I want.
84. My unique talents and gifts bring me an overflow of wealth.
85. My financial success is necessary for my and my family's financial freedom.
86. Money is all around me, and today I will claim my share.
87. I feel free to seek wealth and the freedom it provides.
88. I allow myself to receive more than I ever thought possible.
89. I invite wealth to come to me and when I get it, I hold on to it.
90. I will always be wealthy and financially free.
91. I feel good about the things that I spend my money on.
92. I am able to use my wealth for the

benefit of myself and others around me.
93. I am proud to say that I am financially independent.
94. I always have excess money in my bank accounts and I am constantly attracting more.
95. All of my financial needs are met.
96. I have a portfolio of numerous profitable investments.
97. I have a positive attitude around money, which attracts it to me even more.
98. I completely believe in my ability to create wealth and prosperity.
99. Money comes to me from unexpected places.
100. My income is constantly increasing.
101. I am grateful for the constant flow of money in my life.
102. I have the financial freedom to be

able to make my own choices for my life.
103. I am financially free, and therefore able to do exactly what I want with my life and my time.
104. There is a limitless supply of money and there is more than enough for me and everyone to be rich.
105. I am open to receiving the best life has to offer and attracting the wealth needed to do so.
106. I am committed to acquiring the wealth needed to live my best life possible.
107. My positive thoughts about attracting wealth are coming true.
108. I enjoy making money through the work I do every day.
109. I am comfortable receiving limitless wealth beyond my imagination.

110. The more money I make, the more people I can help.
111. I feel calm and peace, knowing my bills are always paid on time.
112. All of my money making plans work more quickly and easily than I anticipated.
113. I'm surrounded by people who also have a good relationship with money.
114. I am surrounded by other people who also attract money.
115. I believe I possess the ability to be wealthy.
116. I believe I deserve to be wealthy.
117. Anyone and everyone can be financially free and that includes me.
118. I am just as deserving as anyone else to have wealth.
119. I am just as capable of anyone else to create wealth.

120. I am skilled at making money, and it comes easily to me.
121. My personal wealth increases every day in every way.
122. I have the ability and the knowledge to make as much money as I want.
123. My mind remains set on the idea of being wealthy.
124. Being rich is a good thing, and I deserve it just as much as anyone.
125. Large amounts of money will come to me if I am open and receptive.
126. All my thoughts attract wealth.
127. Money naturally seeks me out and stays with me.
128. There is more than enough to go around for everyone.
129. Making a lot of money comes easily to me.
130. I have multiple streams of income that create ultimate freedom for me.

131. I give myself permission to receive and enjoy abundant wealth.
132. I feel relaxed when thinking about my finances because I have abundance.
133. Money comes to me in surprising ways, and I am always on the lookout for it.
134. It is easy for me to make more money and I am good at it.
135. It is possible for me to get all that is possible out of life, and that includes wealth.
136. I am thankful for what I have now and for what is coming to me in the future.
137. I feel happy and calm when I think about my personal finances.
138. I enjoy spending my money to treat myself because I know I have so much more.
139. I enjoy spending my money to

treat my loved ones because I know I have so much more.

140. Generating wealth is simple, and I am great at it.

141. Every time I spend money, it is instantly regenerated with increase.

142. I give my all to whatever I do because I know my efforts always bring me financial reward.

Handling Professional, Work, & Business Stress

1. I am doing my best at work and that is the best that I can do.
2. I am a valuable asset to any professional team.
3. I can get through any project if I just take things one step at a time.
4. The only thing I focus on is the task in front of me right now.
5. I am productive and focused and I easily check things off my to-do list.
6. I have more than enough time to

accomplish the things I need to accomplish.
7. I will find my ideal career and make it mine.
8. I will create my ideal business if that is my desire.
9. My income is always increasing from the work that I do.
10. I radiate energy and confidence when I am at work.
11. My career does not take over my life.
12. Other areas of my life are just as important as the way I make money.
13. I am grateful to have found and realized my professional dreams.
14. The contacts that I need to help me advance professionally are on their way to me.
15. I attract positive mentors who guide me towards success in my chosen field.

16. I am grateful to have a lucrative source of income that supports my dream lifestyle.
17. I am always finding opportunities to grow and expand in my career.
18. I know I will always excel no matter what I do.
19. I am recognized for the quality work I contribute to my field.
20. Even better opportunities are always just around the corner.
21. I am in control of my professional path.
22. I will shape my career to be the way I want it to be.
23. I make great professional connections because I am confident in my abilities.
24. If I decide to change my career, it will lead me to something bigger and better.
25. I am fulfilled by my work.

26. I am challenged by my work in a positive and productive way.
27. I get excited to get to go to work each day.
28. I work with wonderful people who are supportive.
29. I lead my team with humility and grace.
30. I am not afraid to say no because I have faith in my decision making.
31. My career helps me grow into becoming a better person.
32. There is a successful business owner inside me who can manage a business to perfection.
33. I will find my way to the top of any field.
34. I am able to learn any skills I may need to learn in order to get the job done.
35. I bring excellence to every task, no matter how big or small.
36. I am calmly confident in my ability

to manage my business and make it highly successful.
37. Today is the day that opportunity will knock and I will open the door.
38. I perform my work with integrity no matter what.
39. I perform my work with pride no matter what.
40. I perform my work with excellence no matter what.
41. I am wealthy because of the dedicated efforts I have put in.
42. I get closer and closer to my business goals every day.
43. I am successful in my career because I take action.
44. I do what it takes to turn my ideas into reality.
45. I am constantly growing my business and professional income.
46. All of my career success just breeds more success.

47. I am well connected and well respected in my field.
48. I always attract positive thinking people to work with me.
49. I always attract hard working people to work with me.
50. I am always learning new ways to do my work faster and better.
51. My professional efficiency increases every day.
52. I have the ability to be the best in whichever profession I choose.
53. I consciously release any and all negative thoughts that can impede my success.
54. I believe in myself and what I am capable of doing.
55. New opportunities are waiting for me and I am ready to grab them.
56. The best is yet to come for me and my career.
57. Today is going to be a great day at

work and every tomorrow will be too.
58. I am my own best motivator.
59. I capitalize on my opportunities by taking action.
60. I will explore all new avenues to success whenever they present themselves.
61. Each new idea is a gift and I will treat it as such.
62. Every day, I will look for new opportunities for further success.
63. Whenever I need assistance, I can attract the best resources possible to fit my needs.
64. Whenever I need assistance, I can attract the best people possible to fit my needs.
65. Whenever I need assistance, I can attract the best solutions possible to fit my needs.
66. I manage my time efficiently so I can achieve my goals.

67. I am effective at organization, which helps me achieve my goals.
68. I always find a way to enjoy my work.
69. I am grateful to have a means of making great money.
70. I make sure that my values and ambitions work with each other, not against each other.
71. My work surrounds me with inspiring people who push me to do better.
72. I am grateful to work with people who share in my enthusiasm for the work we do.
73. I welcome new work challenges with calm confidence.
74. I am naturally good at finding solutions to problems.
75. I surround myself with people who are highly successful and who encourage me to be the same.

76. I see a new chance for success in every new challenge I face.
77. Overcoming challenges is a way to improve my self-esteem and self-confidence.
78. When obstacles show up, it's a chance for me to show people what I'm made of.
79. I always take time to celebrate my successes and victories.
80. I trust my intuition to help me make wise professional decisions.
81. I am always in tune and intuitively know the best next step to take.
82. Today will bring an abundance of new ideas that I will use to my advantage.
83. I consistently expect winning solutions and I always attract good outcomes.
84. I am happy with my growth in my career and expect more to come in the future.

85. I deserve and demand respect in my career.
86. My career path is the best one for me, no matter what other people are doing.
87. I am steadily climbing the ranks in my field.
88. By being myself, I bring something unique and wonderful to my work.
89. I am a successful person by nature.
90. I will remain consistent in my efforts, and will therefore achieve the results I want.
91. I achieve the goals I set out to achieve.
92. I am ambitious by nature.
93. I have a knack for succeeding at everything I do.
94. I am doing my best at work and that is good enough.

95. I keep my dreams alive with my positive attitude.
96. I always go the extra mile, and it always pays off.
97. I know that my dedication will lead to promotion and increase.
98. I have the energy of a winner because I am a winner.
99. I have the energy of a success because I am a success.
100. I bring joy and light into my workplace with my positive attitude and winning smile.
101. I only speak positively about those that I work with.
102. I have healthy, fulfilling, positive relationships with the people I work with.
103. I speak up boldly and ask intelligent questions when needed.
104. I create my own opportunities and don't just wait for them to come to me.

105. My repertoire of skills is constantly expanding.
106. I put consistent effort and energy into becoming better at what I do.
107. People take notice of my skill and work ethic.
108. I appreciate everyone, both above and below me, who helps contribute to my success.
109. I get what I want in my work by helping other people get what they want.
110. I keep my workspace clean so my mind will be clean.
111. I keep my workspace organized so my mind will be organized.
112. I always see the fruits of my labor.
113. Seeing other people ahead of me simply drives me to be better.
114. I always persist and never quit because things get too hard.
115. I have the wisdom to know when to try a different tactic.

116. I am especially gifted at what I do.
117. I will maintain a positive outlook at work today no matter what happens.
118. Communication with those that I work with is something I do very well.
119. I am only finished with a project when I know it is the best I could have done.
120. The work I do is always done to the best of my ability.
121. I only turn in quality projects, done with care.
122. The people I work with are always happy to see me.
123. I set a great example for other people in my field.
124. I'm always learning, so I can stay relevant in my field.
125. I have the power to make today a good day or a bad day and I

choose to have a good day at work today.
126. All of the work that I do is important and significant.
127. I radiate confidence in my abilities, which gets me noticed.
128. I am open to doing whatever it takes to get the job done.
129. I deserve to be financially stable and I will do what I need to do to get there.
130. I always have the best team to work with.
131. I work with a team of people with unique and valuable skills.
132. I always bring the best out of the people I work with.
133. I am trusted in my field as an honest leader.

Personal Relationships

1. I am grateful to be surrounded by wonderful people who keep me calm and happy.
2. I have a supportive family that makes me feel better in times of stress and anxiety.
3. I have supportive friends that make me feel better in times of stress and anxiety.
4. I take peace in knowing my family is healthy.
5. I take peace in knowing my family is happy.

6. I take peace in knowing my family is safe.
7. I take peace in knowing my friends are healthy.
8. I take peace in knowing my friends are happy.
9. I take peace in knowing my friends are safe.
10. I always attract loving and supportive people into my life.
11. Today, I will create harmony and love in my relationships.
12. The quality of my relationships is always growing.
13. The strength of my relationships is always growing.
14. I'm able to freely express my opinion with the people I love, even if it is different than theirs.
15. I can disagree with the people I love and they still love me.
16. Love is always flowing into me and out from me.

17. People love to spend time with me.
18. I matter to the people in my life and they show me every day how much I matter.
19. I only attract relationships that are good for me.
20. I trust that the right people will come into my life at the right time.
21. I am respected and honored in all of my friendships.
22. I am respected and honored in all of my family relationships.
23. I am respected and honored in my romantic relationship.
24. I am respected and honored in my professional relationships.
25. I am surrounded by people who support me when I need help, any time I ask for it.
26. I know I will always be accepted for who I am.
27. My relationship with myself grows

stronger and deeper every day in every way.
28. It is okay for me to want and need love, and I will get it.
29. True love always finds people when the time is right and the person is right.
30. There is a perfect partner out there for me and I will find them if I haven't already.
31. My partner allows me to be exactly the person I want to be.
32. My needs are met and exceeded in my romantic relationship.
33. My romantic relationship grows stronger and deeper every day in every way.
34. My partner loves me for who I am and does not ask me to be anything I am not.
35. My partner allows me to have personal boundaries and space without feeling threatened.

36. I always have a feeling of safety and security when I am with my partner.
37. I have a partner that treasures the time we spend together.
38. I accept romantic gestures because I deserve to be loved that way.
39. I am worthy of the love and devotion of my caring partner.
40. I am worthy of being everything to that one special person.
41. Every day, I do something to strengthen my relationship with my partner.
42. The special relationship I enjoy with my partner brings me joy and peace.
43. My partner always does things to make me feel special.
44. I trust that I can trust my partner completely.
45. I make time with my partner a priority in my life.

46. I deserve a partner who will love me for who I am.
47. My partner gives me love every day and I cherish our time together.
48. Me and my partner are on the same side.
49. Knowing that my partner loves me fills me with joy.
50. Our relationship is important to both me and my partner and we both cherish it equally.
51. I know that my partner chooses to be with me, which makes me feel secure in our relationship.
52. I deserve to be happy with my partner.
53. I choose to concentrate on all the positive parts of my relationship with my partner.
54. Every day, I become more secure in my partner's love for me.
55. I have learned to love myself and

now I will share that love with those around me.
56. The love I give I will receive; I am confident of that.
57. I only have relationships that are open and honest and have a positive impact on my life.
58. I am better because of the quality of the people in my life.
59. My relationships teach me valuable lessons and skills that make me a better person.
60. I am so happy to have the kind of family that allows me to be the person I need to be.
61. The people in my life teach me to love myself more every day and I am grateful for that.
62. I am always creating wonderful memories in my relationships.
63. I trust the people in my life to make good decisions for themselves.

64. I am open to the ideas of others, and they are open to mine.
65. I am open to the opinions of others, and they are open to mine.
66. I am able to disagree with people and still have a positive relationship with them.
67. I accept the people in my life as they are, the way they do the same for me.
68. I am committed to facilitating the personal and professional growth of the people around me.
69. I willingly help others and willingly receive help.
70. I willingly praise others and willingly receive praise.
71. I give credit where credit is due, as that is no threat to me.
72. I give forgiveness just as freely as I receive it.
73. There is nothing wrong with me

having everything I want to have in my relationships.
74. Love is looking for me right now and I am ready to accept it.
75. I choose my relationships based on what's best for my mental and emotional well-being.
76. I am surrounded by people that love me.
77. I trust my heart to make the right choices.
78. My heart is an amazing thing that gives and receives love for me.
79. I love my family and all that they give to me.
80. I love being able to give to my family.
81. I enjoy being with my friends and I cherish their company.
82. I follow my inner voice and choose relationships that make me happy.
83. My intuition knows what

relationships are best for me and I listen to it.

84. I make it a point to treat other people the way I want them to treat me.
85. I have enough love for myself to make positive relationship choices.
86. I have enough respect for myself to make positive relationship choices.
87. I am able to quickly and gracefully settle disputes in my relationships.
88. My relationships all feature open and honest communication.
89. I do my best to see other people's point of view without judgment.
90. I can share my own opinions without fear of being judged.
91. I recognize that my way is not the only way and my relationships are better for it.
92. I love all the people who are in my life right now and they love me.

93. I deserve respect from other people and I will not settle for anything less.
94. Spending time with my family is something that makes me feel joyous and at peace.
95. I enjoy nurturing my relationships and watching them grow.
96. The caring and loving people I have in my life make me more caring and loving.
97. I can easily apologize when I am wrong.
98. I choose only those relationships that fulfill me and lift me up.
99. I accept other people for who they are and appreciate them for what they do.
100. I am fully open and honest with the people in my life.
101. I always try to make other people feel important when they are with me.

102. When I find great people to work with, I always make them feel valued.
103. The people around me believe in me and support me fully.
104. I value giving love and receiving love and I make both a priority in my life.
105. I always choose love and light.
106. I have enough confidence to not worry about my relationships.
107. I will leave the past in the past and only accept loving relationships in the future.
108. I have a high level of self-worth, which is evident by the quality of people I allow in my life.
109. My relationship with my partner allows me to be happy and carefree.
110. I am a trustworthy person and I attract trustworthy people.

111. I trust that the people in my life want what's best for me.
112. I am always becoming a happier and more secure person.
113. I put my relationship with myself first and it pays off.
114. My confidence and self-assurance come from me, not my relationships.
115. The problems of my past relationships do not plague my current relationships.
116. Good quality relationships take work that I am willing to put in.
117. I make consistent effort to show people how much I care.
118. I make consistent effort to show people how much I love them.
119. I enjoy the warmth and love that being with my family makes me feel.
120. I choose to see the best in people.

121. I am able to solve problems in a collaborative fashion.
122. I solve issues in a way where everyone wins.
123. I am able to get through any argument in any relationship.
124. My relationships always come out better on the other side of disagreement.
125. It is easy for me to talk about my feelings with people.
126. I leave the past in the past and focus on moving forward in the future.
127. I am supported in my career by people who value my work and help my talents shine.

Overcoming Social Anxiety

1. I confidently smile at strangers.
2. I am constantly meeting new and exciting people every day.
3. I always make good first impressions.
4. Everyone I encounter sees me in a positive light.
5. I feel comfortable speaking in front of small and large groups of people because I know my thoughts and opinions are valuable.

6. I am confident in being the first person to start a conversation.
7. Everyone I meet and come across is glad to meet me.
8. People are attracted to my magnetic charm, personality, and intelligence.
9. I have a natural gift for making people feel welcome and comfortable around me.
10. I feel very comfortable in new social situations, and I love meeting new people.
11. The art of conversation is a skill that I am great at.
12. I confidently make eye contact with everyone I come across.
13. I remain calm, confident, and outspoken, even when faced with a large group of people.
14. I have many gifts to offer to the world and people are happy to see me.

15. I have a beautiful spirit that people naturally gravitate towards.
16. I confidently join conversations that are already in progress.
17. I happily say yes to event invitations even when I don't know anyone else who is going.
18. I walk up to groups of people with confidence.
19. I regularly take the time to meet new people and make new friends.
20. I love meeting new people and learning about them.
21. There are many interesting thoughts in my head that people would love to hear.
22. I am engaging and charming in conversation.
23. Being around other people makes me feel happy and energized.
24. I fearlessly go to parties and events because I know people will like me.

25. People enjoy my company and my presence is a gift.
26. I am graciously accept the compliments that I constantly receive.
27. I feel calm and confident in all social situations.
28. I feel completely okay with being myself at all times.
29. I love what I see in the mirror and I am confident in the way I look.
30. My thoughts are interesting and other people enjoy hearing them.
31. My opinions are valuable and other people enjoy hearing them.
32. I can talk to anyone I want to with ease and sincerity.
33. I have an inner peace in social situations that radiates to everyone around me.
34. Love and compassion allow me to connect with other people on a deeper level.

35. I fully trust in my ability to shine in the world today.
36. I have the power to be confident today and I will do so.
37. I connect with people easily and enjoy talking to them.
38. There is something good in everyone and I always find it.
39. I am completely comfortable walking up to strangers and starting conversation.
40. My calmness and confidence in social situations is so strong, it makes other people feel at ease.
41. I am always comfortable being myself on dates and in romantic situations.
42. I am always comfortable being myself in conversation regardless of how the other person acts or feels.
43. I am likeable and charming to everyone I meet.

44. I remain humble and kind, even though I am constantly being flooded with compliments.
45. Today I am more confident than I was yesterday, and tomorrow I will be more confident than I am today.
46. I believe that I have countless positive qualities to offer to any relationship.
47. I am grateful for the good friends I have now and for the ones I have yet to meet.
48. Good things always come when I put myself out there.
49. I have a healthy, fun, and thriving social life.
50. I am able to be around new people easily.
51. My ability to always be myself no matter what, is inspiring to others.
52. I am great at finding things in common with people.

53. I am great at making people feel welcome and easing their social anxiety.
54. Parties and social gatherings make me feel excited and energized.
55. I always look forward to opportunities to meet new people.
56. I enjoy sharing my personality with the world.
57. I am always graceful and poised in social situations.
58. People say I am a confident person, so I must be one.
59. I have many good qualities that I am ready and willing to share with others.
60. People can sense all the great things I have to offer, and people want to meet me.
61. I am friendly and engaging when people approach me.
62. I maintain a positive attitude in

conversations no matter what the other person's attitude is.
63. I maintain a cheerful and upbeat disposition in conversation no matter the other person's disposition is.
64. I will always be myself whether other people accept it or not.
65. I am completely myself in social interactions whether I receive cues that the other person likes me or not.
66. I bring my complete personality to social interactions whether I receive cues that the other person likes it or not.
67. I proudly and confidently share my opinions when appropriate whether I receive cues that other people agree with me or not.
68. Approaching strangers is easy and fun for me.

69. Approaching strangers comes naturally for me.
70. Starting conversation is easy and fun for me.
71. Starting conversation comes naturally for me.
72. I always have endless interesting topics to talk about in conversation.
73. It is easy for me to make eye contact with other people.
74. I get excited to meet new people because something good always comes from forming new relationships.
75. I love to go out with people and do fun activities with them.
76. I am constantly trying new things.
77. I love opportunities that get me outside of my comfort zone.
78. I am effortlessly witty and charming in conversation.
79. I can easily and comfortably hang

out with other people and have fun doing nothing.
80. I easily and comfortably enjoy and appreciate moments of silence in conversation.
81. I am comfortable in moments of silence because I know my presence is enough.
82. I like to be around other people because they give me energy.
83. I have a strong and powerful positive presence that energizes and excites others.
84. Making conversation with new people is something I do easily and naturally.
85. I can maintain a feeling of calm when I am in a new situation.
86. I am relaxed when I am at parties and I always enjoy myself.
87. New situations are new chances to see and do new things.

88. I jump into conversations with ease and confidence.
89. Speaking in public is something I do well, and people always like what I have to say.
90. I look forward to opportunities to speak in public.
91. I will gladly do an activity in public even when I don't have another person to do it with.
92. I am comfortable attending events by myself because I know I will always make friends when I get there.
93. I equally enjoy my quality time spent alone and with others.
94. People see that I am comfortable being myself, which makes them feel more comfortable too.
95. Everywhere I go, people are excited to meet me.
96. I have high self-esteem, and I am worthy of everything I have.

97. I have accomplished and experienced great things in my life that are worthy of sharing.
98. I take advantage of every opportunity I get to do something fun, even if it means doing it by myself.
99. I am an interesting and intriguing person, and people love conversing with me.
100. I have a very interesting life that people love to hear about.
101. I have so many wonderful things to offer and I will begin today.
102. Speaking up is my right and my duty, and people want to hear what I have to say.
103. I am full of creativity and great ideas.
104. I have amazing social skills that other people admire.
105. I love my confident and outgoing

demeanor, and I share it with others.

106. Where ever I go, I am always well received.
107. People look forward to events when they know that I am coming.
108. My presence is wanted and appreciated.
109. My voice is wanted and appreciated.
110. Having sharp social skills is an improvement to my overall quality of life.
111. I am a fun and interesting person and I attract other people who are fun and interesting too.
112. People take me seriously when I speak my mind.
113. I always intuitively know the right words to say.
114. I always intuitively know the right way to say things.
115. When I open my mouth to speak,

the right words flow out effortlessly.

116. People always listen to me with their undivided attention.
117. When I have something important to say, my voice is strong, confident, and unwavering.
118. I can go to events alone and leave with a new friend.
119. Having a social life is very important and enjoyable for me.
120. Trying new things makes me feel good so I will try one new thing today.
121. I speak up and defend myself when necessary because I am worthy of being defended.
122. I view my past social mistakes with amusement and learn from them for the future.
123. It gets easier and easier for me to talk to people every day.
124. I am constantly throwing myself

into new social situations and it gets more easy and comfortable every time.
125. If I do not enjoy the direction a conversation is going, I start a new one or leave.
126. My heart overflows with happiness today and I must share that happiness with other people.
127. I am strong and bold and I walk into every room with my head held high.
128. I am completely the person I want to be and others accept me for it.
129. The uncertainty of new social situations and events excites me.
130. I am an attractive person inside and out, and other people want to get to know me.
131. I exude magnetic confidence where ever I go at all times.
132. I am aware of my potential and I

will share my potential with other people today.
133. I make the world a better place every day just by being in it.
134. I deserve compliments and I give and receive them with grace.
135. I am confident, yet humble.
136. I possess all the social skills I need to face any social situation I find myself in.
137. I maintain my inner peace despite any external conflict.
138. I can disagree with someone with grace and confidence.
139. I have an interesting life and valuable opinions worthy of sharing on social media if I choose to.
140. When I choose to share on social media, my content uplifts and inspires others.
141. I only follow social media accounts that make me feel good.

142. I have much to offer other people and I will bring it today.
143. I openly share my ideas and creativity in professional situations.
144. When I have questions, I speak up and ask them.
145. Other people see and admire my success and confidence and want to emulate me.
146. I am terrific at making new friends and social connections.
147. I attract people who push me to be a better person.
148. I attract people who are moral, ethical, and honest.
149. I attract people who are confident, energizing, and fun to be around.
150. The relationships I attract are always mutually beneficial.
151. I am a good influence on other people, and other people are a good influence on me.

152. I feel complete and worthy with my own self-validation.
153. Other people see that I believe in myself and it makes them believe in me too.
154. I always find a way to brighten a stranger's day by smiling and speaking to them.
155. I make my own decisions and think for myself.
156. I openly share my real self with everyone at all times.
157. I attract happy people because I am a happy person.
158. I am kind to others and seek out opportunities to comfort people who are lonely.
159. The way I see myself is far more important than the way other people see me.
160. My opinion of myself is the most important opinion there is.

Physical Body & Health

1. I have earned time for rest and I will enjoy it without guilt.
2. I always put good things in my body, and in turn I always get good things out.
3. I will do whatever I need to do in order to make myself feel better today.
4. Exercise is my way of showing my body how much I love it.
5. My body is perfect for me right now while I work to make it better.

6. I can make my body into whatever I want or need it to be.
7. My body is a machine and I fuel it with healthy food that makes it work better for me.
8. I possess self-control over my eating, which carries over into self-control over my life.
9. I effortlessly carry out a healthy lifestyle and eat healthy with ease.
10. I am easily able to say no to distracting, nagging cravings.
11. I am proud of the way I am taking care of my body inside and out.
12. My body is free of drugs and substances so that my mind can be free and in my control.
13. Every day I say no to bad choices is another day closer to a healthy life.
14. I feel more love for myself than I feel for my impulses.
15. I rest well at night, which gives me

the strength to fight my battles during the day.
16. My immune system is strong and capable of fighting any and every disease.
17. I consistently and effortlessly make wise choices for my body, and I can see and feel the difference.
18. I enjoy taking good care of myself.
19. I keep my body strong, which keeps my mind strong.
20. My body is a powerful, self-healing machine.
21. I allow myself time to feel better and recover when needed.
22. I deserve to live a healthy, pain-free life and I do what I need to do to achieve that.
23. I am dedicated to my journey of always improving my health.
24. I think only healthy thoughts about my body.

25. The positive state of my body makes it easy for me to maintain a positive state of mind.
26. I choose to love my body the way it is while I work to make it better from the inside out.
27. I am blessed to be able to move and exercise at will.
28. I am proud of the body that I have worked to create.
29. I am always looking for ways to improve my life and my well-being.
30. I focus on what is right with my body while I fix what needs fixing.
31. I have the power to get stronger and stronger every day.
32. I am full of vitality and unstoppable inner power.
33. I have the energy I need to conquer each day.
34. I alone hold the power to make myself as healthy as I want to be.

35. I am grateful that I woke up this morning with a new opportunity to create my life into what I want it to be.
36. My body may be under construction, but I am making great progress.
37. I am dedicated to making the temple that I live in as strong and healthy as it can possibly be.
38. I recognize that I only get one body and I treat it with respect and love.
39. I am constantly learning how to take better care of myself.
40. My body is capable of miracles.
41. Positive thoughts yield positive results in my health journey.
42. My energy levels are increasing each and every day.
43. I focus my energy on improving my body.
44. I look good because I feel good,

and I feel good because I look good.
45. I take care of myself and take pride in my appearance.
46. I am mentally and physically strong enough to overcome any physical challenge my body could face.
47. I am in control of my body and I choose what I put in it.
48. I make wise decisions when it comes to my health, and see and feel the benefits.
49. I love every part of my body and am grateful for the working vessel that I live in.
50. Every part of me is beautiful.
51. I always do what is within my power to improve my body, while letting go of things I can't control.
52. The way that I feel matters above all else, so I put effort into doing things that make me feel better.

53. When I think good thoughts, I feel good.
54. I am at peace with the way my body looks.
55. My body has the strength to get me through any challenge.
56. I take care of myself because I am the only me I will ever have.

Cultivating Optimism

1. I know that everything will work out for my good in the end.
2. I have a future that is exciting and full of hope.
3. Worrying about a situation does not affect its outcome, so I choose not to worry.
4. I have the power to see the good in any situation and turn any circumstance around.
5. I will begin today with a feeling of unshakable optimism.

6. I expect to find success in everything I do today.
7. I choose to feel capable, confident, and optimistic in every situation.
8. I am happy and excited about what today will bring me.
9. I only have room in my mind for positive and optimistic thoughts.
10. Things are always working behind the scenes for my benefit, even when I cannot see it.
11. Life has amazing things to offer and they are on their way to me.
12. I will achieve every goal that I set out to achieve.
13. Even in the darkest times, I still see the light up ahead.
14. I have a naturally optimistic state of being.
15. I spread happiness and hope to everyone around me today and every day.

16. All of my experiences in life are rewarding and enriching.
17. Practicing positivity is a priority in my life.
18. My future is full of excitement.
19. Every new day brings me exciting new experiences.
20. I embrace challenges as opportunities to grow and become better.
21. Every morning, I am eager to see what new miracles will happen today.
22. Every day, I am closer to meeting my goals.
23. I am more positive than ever before about myself and the prospects for my future.
24. I am constantly attracting amazing opportunities.
25. I am happier today than I was yesterday and I expect to be even happier tomorrow.

26. My life improves more and more, every day in every way.
27. Everything in my life is working out for my benefit.
28. I become more optimistic every moment of every day.
29. I feel a state of calm and peace when thinking about my life.
30. The events in my life are happening exactly as they should right now.
31. Good things always happen to me because I always expect good things to happen to me.
32. I deserve the best, and therefore, I expect the best.
33. I expect the best, and therefore I receive the best.
34. Wonderful things happen to me every day and I am happy to welcome them into my life.
35. My spirit is overflowing with enthusiasm and optimism.

36. The best possible outcome will always happen.
37. I choose to focus on the positivity of now and the optimism of the future.
38. I always find humor in all situations and find the best side of things.
39. I have a fantastic future ahead of me.
40. I love my life, past, present, and future.
41. I always seek and find the bright side no matter what.
42. There is always a silver lining, and I will always be the one to find it.
43. No matter what happens, I will remain optimistic and positive.
44. I feel wonderful about myself and my place in life.
45. It is easy for me to radiate positive energy and to think positive thoughts.

46. From the very moment I wake up, I am full of positive thoughts.
47. Other people are drawn to me because I am full of optimism and positivity.
48. Even during times of difficulty or stress, I am able to think positive thoughts.
49. I can switch my mind to a positive wavelength, any time, on command.
50. Thinking in a positive manner is a natural part of my being.
51. I will only think positive thoughts no matter what happens to me.
52. I will always work to find positive elements in every situation.
53. My life is improving all the time.
54. My tendency to think in a positive manner uplifts all the people around me.
55. I am someone who naturally feels positive all the time.

56. I enjoy the power of positive thinking and it comes naturally to me.
57. Every day, my thoughts grow more positive and optimistic.
58. Optimistic thoughts enrich my life with wonderful possibilities.
59. I am so mentally strong that I have unshakeable peace of mind.
60. I firmly believe my dreams will be a reality one day.
61. When I fulfill my dreams, they will be even better than I ever imagined.
62. My future looks bright and beautiful.
63. I look forward to a life full of infinite possibilities.
64. I love feeling hopeful about what will happen in my future.
65. I'm at peace because I know greater things are ahead.

66. Things always go well for me because they are supposed to.
67. I appreciate every moment of every day.
68. I can accomplish anything I want to if I am optimistic enough.
69. I am successful in whatever I do because I accept nothing less.
70. I solve problems using creativity and positivity to ensure a good outcome.
71. I can find a solution to every problem because I don't quit searching until I do.
72. My positivity is a powerful force that makes me unstoppable.
73. Everything I do turns into a success because I won't stop until it does.
74. I truly believe in my abilities and skills.
75. I am certain all things will work for me.

76. I possess all the things I need to succeed and I will use them with enthusiasm.
77. My strength is much greater than any challenge I will face today.
78. There is no mountain that I do not have the ability to conquer.
79. I make my own success.
80. I go through my life with self-assurance and confidence in my abilities.
81. I am more than capable, and confident I will achieve my goals.
82. I will realize all my dreams, sooner rather than later.
83. I am fearless in the face of every obstacle.
84. I will learn everything I can from every situation I face.
85. I woke up with all I need to have a great day.
86. I am fully driven to achieve my goals.

87. My life is a gift and I appreciate it greatly.
88. I fill my life with positive people and we bring out the best in each other.
89. I release all negative thoughts and leave room only for optimism and positivity.
90. My outer well-being is matched by my inner harmony and peace.
91. My happiness comes from within me.
92. My cheerful spirit is contagious to those around me.
93. I am proud of all the things I have accomplished and will accomplish in the future.
94. I have a clear and compelling image in my mind of the amazing person I will become.
95. Realizing my dreams is only a matter of time.

96. Positivity is a choice, and it is what I always choose.
97. I have no worries because I am totally at peace with myself and my life.
98. My confidence is soaring daily because I know what I am worth.
99. I choose to love myself and to be completely happy.
100. My words and actions directly reflect my positive attitude.
101. I am led by my dreams, not my fears.
102. I use my good energy to spread good in the world.
103. I am empowered, not crippled, by my circumstances.
104. The responsibility for my happiness lies in my own hands.
105. I enjoy a life of purpose and passion.
106. I am happy with the things I have

and I will appreciate them while I get more.

107. My past is in the past and I look happily towards my future.

All by Drew McArthur on Amazon & Audible

Affirmations, Meditation, & Hypnosis For Positivity & A Success Mindset:

Power Of Thought To Create A Millionaire Mind, Manifest Wealth, Abundance, Better Relationships, & Form Positive Habits Now

Rewire Your Brain Affirmations, Meditation, & Hypnosis For Confidence, Motivation, & Discipline:

Increase Focus, Productivity, Willpower, Self Esteem, & Eliminate Distraction & Procrastination Habits

Step-By-Step Motivational Goal Setting Course For Life Mastery:

How To Change Your Brain, Set Your Vision, And Get Everything You Want To Have Your Best Year Ever

Monkey Mind Cure Affirmations, Meditation & Hypnosis:

How to Stop Worrying, Kill Fear, Rewire Your Brain, and Change Your Anxious Thoughts to Start Living a Stress and Anxiety-Free Life

Think Happy Thoughts: Affirmations and Meditation for Positive Thinking, Learned Optimism and a Happy Brain

Unlock the Advantage of the Happiness Habit and Project the Power of Positive Energy

Millionaire Money Mindset: Affirmations, Meditation, & Hypnosis

Using Positive Thinking Psychology to Train Your Mind to Grow Wealth, Think like the New Rich and Take the Secret Fastlane to Success